The Frog
Natural Acrobat

text and photos by Paul Starosta

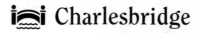

Charlesbridge

Library of Congress Cataloging-in-Publication Data
Starosta, Paul.
  [Grenouille, parfaite acrobate. English]
  The frog, natural acrobat / text and photographs by Paul
Starosta.
     p.   cm. — (Animal close-ups)
  Summary: Examines the physical characteristics and habits of
frogs.
  ISBN 0-88106-437-8 (softcover)
  1. Frogs—Juvenile literature. [1. Frogs.] I. Title. II. Series.
QL668.E2S73913 1996   95-46393
  597.8'9—dc20

Photographs copyright © 1991 by Paul Starosta: covers;
pp. 3-25; p. 26, top right and bottom left
Copyright © 1991 by Éditions Milan
300, rue Léon-Joulin, 31101 Toulouse Cedex 100, France
Original edition first published by Éditions Milan under the title *la grenouille, parfaite acrobate*
French series editor, Valérie Tracqui
Translated by Timothy Froggatt

Printed in Korea
10   9   8   7   6   5   4   3   2

Night noise

Night falls on the pond. The ducks that lived here all winter long have already migrated for the spring and summer. Now, the marsh will be calm again. Only the reeds move, blown by wind that brushes softly by them. But suddenly: Croak, Croak, Croak!

The noise grows louder. The croaking is so loud that it can be heard hundreds of yards away. It is not an elephant crashing through the reeds— it is only a little tree frog singing his mating song.

Crooooak! No other male will approach him. Without moving, other singers raise their voices from the bushes nearby. In these first few days of spring, no female tree frogs are to be found. They are still sleeping. . . .

What a loud noise from such a little frog. The tree frog is only about two inches long, the size of a small egg.

Only the male tree frog sings. He can be distinguished from the female by his expandable throat.

The male tree frog has one large vocal sac under his chin.

The tree frog's nostrils and eyes are on top of its head. Like the crocodile, when the tree frog is in the water, only the top of its head stays above the surface.

Moonlight romance

The nighttime concerts continue. At the end of a few days, the first female tree frogs finally appear. For the first time in months, they jump into the water. The males increase their efforts to grab the attention of the females. They inflate their throat pouches as much as possible. These pouches serve as echo chambers to amplify their songs. In the water, where the competition is fierce, they can croak for hours without stopping.

The male tree frog uses his voice to attract a mate and to keep his rivals away. A female is nearby. When she is close enough, he moves toward her.

Like the toad, tree frogs mate in the water. They begin mating when they are about two years old.

Like a fish in water

The little female frog quickly produces a sac of eggs, which is immediately fertilized by the male. Within only a couple of hours, more than eight hundred eggs begin their dangerous lives in the water.

The eggs are the size of little pearls.

Inside each, an embryo begins to develop.

A greedy newt gobbles up the eggs of one frog.

The little cluster of eggs is left alone among the algae. It is at the mercy of hungry creatures. Fortunately, after two weeks many eggs survive. Soon, out of each egg comes a small larva. The larva has no mouth or visible external organs. It stays fixed to the covering of its egg by a sucker.

At birth, the larvae cannot move and are very vulnerable. Underwater they breathe through gills.

A few days later, the tadpole is still very small. But it already has a mouth, and it has begun to move by wiggling its tail.

Soon, gills begin to appear on each side of the larva's head. A tail begins to sprout, a mouth forms, and the gills become covered by skin. Its sense of smell has developed and so have its organs for sensing vibrations in the water.

The tadpole, a little fish without scales, is well equipped as it sets out to conquer its small world.

To eat, the tadpole uses its hard, hornlike lips. Its tiny hind legs are already visible.

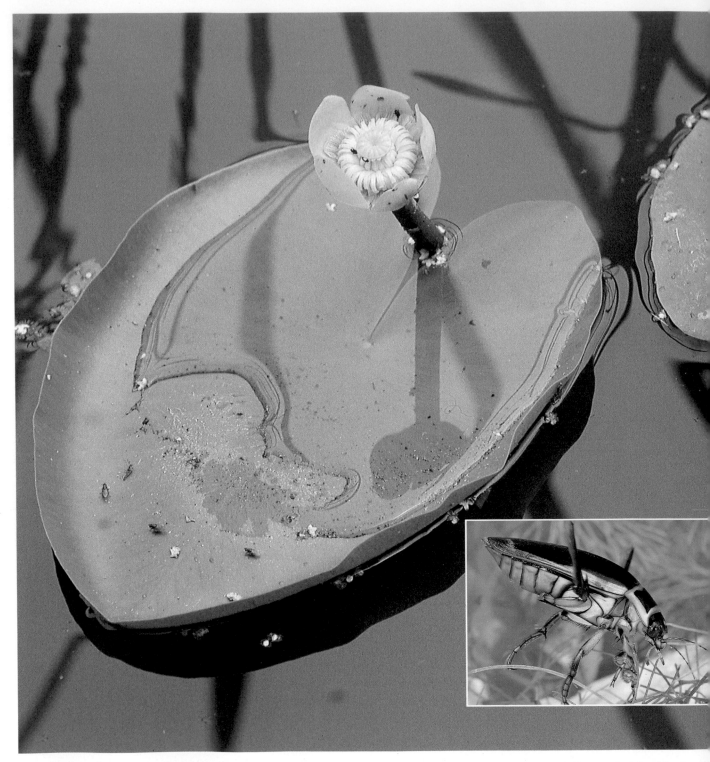

Below the surface of the water, the tadpoles continue to develop.

Against a quick, well-armed water beetle, the tadpole has little chance of survival.

While the tadpole's hind legs finish growing, its front legs begin to develop under the skin.

A few months later, all four of the tadpole's legs are formed. Then it stops eating and begins to absorb its tail, which is full of important nutrients.

The tail has not completely disappeared, but the tadpole's lungs are already working.

The metamorphosis

It is not hard for the tadpoles to find something to eat in the water. All around them, the vegetation is like a forest.

The change from tadpoles into frogs continues. While they eat, they keep growing. They are able to push themselves with their hind legs, then with their front legs. Their tails continue to shrink, and their gills have already disappeared. Now, the tadpoles breathe through their new lungs and must swim to the surface for air. By the time they are about two-and-a-half months old, many of the tree frog's eggs have grown into little amphibians with four feet.

But this place can be dangerous, too. It is home to the ferocious water beetle and the larvae of the dragonfly. Some tadpoles will get eaten while the others continue to grow.

Eyes as big as its stomach

Some young tree frogs prefer to stay on the banks of the pond or in the reeds so they can breathe comfortably. But what a treat they make for a grass snake! The snake quickly swallows several frogs whole. There are always some that survive, though, and continue to discover their new world.

The frog has a wide range of vision. Its eyes are specially adapted for aquatic life.

The tree frog rests on a lily pad before returning to the banks of the pond.

The banks of the pond are also home to the grass snake, a threat to the young frogs.

A young fly has landed on the stem of a plant. A hungry tree frog exploring the grass quickly catches it and eats it. This is the first meal of its new diet. The frog has lost its sense of smell, which is of little use in spotting mosquitoes and other insects, but it has gained ears that detect the humming of its new prey. The heat of the sun is beginning to dry out its skin, so the tree frog goes to hide in a moist, shady place.

The female tree frog lays between 800 and 1,000 eggs at one time. This makes for a very busy pond bank!

Breathing through the skin

It is raining. Hundreds of little frogs leave their hiding places. On these first days of July, rain is very rare. The frogs must take advantage of it. Not only does the rain keep their skin from drying out, it is also a way for them to quench their thirst. The tree frog does not need to open its mouth wide to drink. It only needs to sit in the rain and the water will be absorbed by its skin.

Oxygen also passes into the frog's blood directly through its skin. The frog's lungs have to do very little work. It is easy to see why this amphibian shelters its delicate skin from the burning sun.

The tree frog grips the stem of a plant with its eight fingers and ten toes.

Blood vessels under the frog's skin take in most of its oxygen.

Over time, the frog's skin begins to make a sticky substance that keeps it moist all the time. The frog also secretes a poison that kills parasites and irritates the mouths of hungry predators. Its skin contains the pigments that give the frog its beautiful colors.

Growing bigger

The little tree frog grows bigger. Unlike children, the tree frog does not eat peanut butter and jelly. Its favorite meal is an appetizer of mosquitoes, a main course of ants and little spiders, and some beetles for dessert.

When night arrives, the tree frog becomes alert and begins to hunt.

The acrobatic frog jumps into the air and attaches itself to a branch or a leaf with the damp, sticky suction cups on its fingers and toes.

To protect itself, the ant produces a poisonous acid, but this does not stop the hungry frog.

As long as it remains still, the spider has nothing to fear. But if it moves, it will be spotted quickly.

This tree frog just swallowed its prey, and its mouth is already closed air tight.

Thanks to its two long, folded hind legs, which it can release like springs, the tree frog can jump on anything that moves. It only attacks prey that is smaller than it is or that it can chew. The tree frog has miniature teeth in its upper jaw and on the roof of its mouth. When other small creatures are plentiful, the tree frog will grow quickly.

As it gets bigger, the tree frog does not fear the sun as much as it did when it was young. It begins to venture into the trees.

Little tree frogs attack mosquitoes and ants. Big tree frogs gobble up earwigs and other bugs.

A chameleon without a tail

Tree frogs can live for about seven or eight years. Once they are fully grown, they can defend themselves from hungry predators.

With a suction cup at the end of each finger and toe, they can jump easily from branch to branch without slipping.

Tree frogs also have an excellent camouflage. Their skin can change from green to brown to gray depending on the color of their surroundings.

Tree frogs' front legs are short and have four long fingers with suction cups at the ends.

The tree frog's skin is usually green and smooth on its back and brown and grainy on its stomach.

Whether in the trees or on the water's banks, storks love frogs.

he tree frog swims the breaststroke expertly.

During the day the tree frog sleeps in the sun, securely attached to a leaf, the stem of a reed, or a branch. Every once in a while, when the heat of the sun gets too strong, it refreshes itself in the pond. With its strong palms and hind legs, it swims very well. After its swim, the frog returns to its tree. This is its domain.

Hibernation

It is almost autumn. Bad weather is approaching. The tree frog hunts in the daylight during these final warm hours at the end of summer. Finally, when the frog can no longer stay warm enough, it looks for some shelter in which to sleep. A cracked rock, dead leaves, or a hole in a tree will protect it from the harshness of winter. Its breathing slows down as it begins to hibernate, but it continues to absorb oxygen through its skin.

The tree frog stops eating and drinking. In a deep sleep, it will remain hidden until the first signs of spring. When spring arrives, it will wake up and start its activities again.

Well hidden in the nook of a reed, the little tree frog takes advantage of the last rays of sun.

20

A tree frog takes shelter to avoid freezing to death. It remains completely motionless and breathes only through its skin.

Danger

Like other amphibians, tree frogs suffer from pollution and the development of wetlands. In addition, they are often run over by cars, and their legs are considered a delicacy in some parts of the world. Some populations of tree frogs are endangered, but in a few countries they are protected by law.

Pollution gauge

Some superstitious people put tree frogs in jars with small ladders to predict the weather. This is as cruel as it is useless. Tree frogs do not forecast the weather, but they and all other amphibians do help tell us about the state of our planet's health. Their eggs are very sensitive to water pollution and their fine skin absorbs toxic gases as well as oxygen. The fact that their numbers are dwindling throughout the world is very disturbing.

A bad taste

The trend of eating frog legs as a delicacy has caused many frogs to be killed. Each year, millions of them are captured. Killing these frogs disturbs a natural balance. When the frogs are no longer around to eat insects, more insects survive. To get rid of the insects, people spread insecticides, but these poisons kill the remaining frogs. They also wipe out fish that eat many of the insects. In the end, without the amphibians or the fish, the insects adapt and multiply.

Particularly sensitive to air and water pollution, frogs are indicators of the planet's health.

Millions of the frog legs that are eaten come from green frogs taken from the wild, especially in Asia and Eastern Europe. Frogs are not bred for this purpose.

Millions of victims on the roads!

When it is time to reproduce, toads want to find their native ponds. If their ponds are on the other side of roads, they will try to reach them by hopping through traffic. In some areas, tunnels, or "toadways," have been put under the roads to help reduce this killing. These initiatives, although very localized, help make drivers more sensitive to the problem and save the lives of many toads.

Frogs need water.

"Don't eat them and try not to crush them." This is the saying of those who try to protect frogs. One way to help save frogs is to create a pond in your yard or at your school. Do not put fish in your pond, since they will eat the frogs' eggs and larvae. An entire population of amphibians will soon take over the pond and provide opportunities for many wonderful observations.

Working with a few friends, you can dig a hole for a pond quickly.

Other frogs and toads

In prehistoric times, fish left the sea to become frogs and other amphibians: toads, newts, salamanders. . . .

Even though they have lost their scales, the current species of amphibians still need moisture. Their larvae live in the water, and they are cold-blooded—their body temperature varies with their environment. Frogs are part of the Anura order of amphibians, those that have no tails. Their bodies are squat, and their hind legs, which are adapted to jumping, are more or less webbed.

The little *midwife toads* live in masses of fallen rocks, old walls, and even in cities, but they are never far from water. The male has a song that sounds like a flute. After mating, he transports the eggs—usually about sixty of them— by piling them up on his hind legs. He will put them in the water when it is time for them to hatch.

▲

Like tree frogs, *pelodytids* are only about two inches long and the males attract their mates by croaking. They spend most of their time on land and are very active, jumping and climbing in the vegetation.

▶

▲ Active in the day as well as at night, *green frogs* are very aquatic. They stay warm on the riverbanks but are always ready to go for a swim. They hibernate underwater in the mud.

Some *toads* do not have expandable throats to amplify their songs. To hear them, you have to be very close. The males are smaller than the females. At night, they eat slugs, snails, and insects, which makes gardeners very happy. ▶

Exotic frogs

The order Anura includes more than 3,000 species that are found all over the world, except in the polar regions. The tropical species are very colorful. Whether they live in the trees, on the ground, or in the water, their behavior is similar.

▲
Mantellins are only about one inch long. They live on the ground and leave their eggs in holes. After hatching, their larvae are swept into the water by rainstorms.

The long fingers with suction-cup tips of the *rhacophorids* help these frogs live in the trees. During the egg-laying season, they make nests of foam that hang over water. When tadpoles leave the nests, they fall into the water below them. ▼

Dendrobatins, or *poison arrow frogs,* are small and very colorful. They live in the tropical forests of Central and South America, where people of the region use their venom to poison the tips of arrows.

Microhylids live all over the world, except in Europe. They usually eat ants or termites. Some of them even live in the termites' nests, where they devour the occupants.